EMMANUEL JOSEPH

Code of the Heart, Balancing Love, Career, and Faith in the Age of AI

Copyright © 2025 by Emmanuel Joseph

All rights reserved. No part of this publication may be reproduced, stored or transmitted in any form or by any means, electronic, mechanical, photocopying, recording, scanning, or otherwise without written permission from the publisher. It is illegal to copy this book, post it to a website, or distribute it by any other means without permission.

First edition

This book was professionally typeset on Reedsy. Find out more at reedsy.com

Contents

1 Chapter 1   1

1

Chapter 1

Chapter 1: The Dawn of AI and Its Impact on Human Connection In an age where artificial intelligence permeates every facet of life, the question of its impact on human connection becomes paramount. The rapid evolution of AI technology has reshaped how we communicate, work, and even fall in love. Once unimaginable conveniences are now everyday realities, but they come with a new set of challenges. As we integrate AI into our daily routines, we must grapple with the potential loss of genuine human interaction and the essence of what makes us human.

AI's influence on relationships cannot be understated. With dating apps and virtual assistants facilitating our social lives, the art of human connection is being redefined. While technology can bring people together, it can also create a barrier, a screen between two souls. The authenticity of face-to-face conversations and the warmth of a genuine smile risk becoming lost in the digital noise. Navigating this new terrain requires a mindful approach, ensuring that the heart remains at the center of our interactions.

Career landscapes are also undergoing a transformation, as AI automates tasks and redefines roles. The promise of increased productivity and innovation is tantalizing, but it comes with a caveat. As machines take on more responsibilities, the human workforce must adapt, learning new skills and finding new ways to add value. The balance between leveraging AI's capabilities and preserving human creativity and empathy becomes a delicate dance, one that demands continuous learning and adaptability.

Faith, in this new age, faces its own set of challenges and opportunities. Spirituality and religious practices, often grounded in tradition and human connection, must find a place in a world dominated by technology. AI can be a tool for spreading faith and fostering community, but it can also lead to a sense of isolation if not used mindfully. As we navigate this brave new world, maintaining a sense of purpose and connection to something greater than ourselves is essential.

Chapter 2: Love in the Digital Age Love, the timeless force that drives humanity, finds itself at a crossroads in the digital age. The advent of AI and digital platforms has revolutionized how we seek and sustain romantic relationships. Online dating has become a ubiquitous part of modern courtship, offering endless possibilities and instant connections. However, this convenience can sometimes come at the expense of depth and authenticity, as swipes and algorithms replace chance encounters and heartfelt conversations.

In this new era, love stories are often written in code, with AI-powered matchmakers predicting compatibility based on data points and preferences. While these technological advancements can enhance our ability to find compatible partners, they can also lead to a transactional approach to relationships. The challenge lies in striking a balance between leveraging technology to find love and nurturing the emotional connections that make relationships meaningful.

As we navigate the digital landscape of love, maintaining open communication and emotional intimacy becomes paramount. Text messages and video calls can bridge physical distances, but they cannot fully replace the warmth of a touch or the comfort of a shared silence. In this age of instant gratification, patience and genuine effort are key to cultivating lasting relationships. Embracing vulnerability and authenticity in our digital interactions can help us forge deeper connections, transcending the limitations of technology.

Moreover, the digital age offers opportunities for love to flourish in new ways. Long-distance relationships, once fraught with challenges, can now thrive with the help of technology. Virtual reality dates, shared playlists, and collaborative projects can keep couples connected despite miles apart. As we embrace these innovations, we must also remember to prioritize quality time and meaningful experiences, ensuring that technology enhances rather than replaces the essence of love.

Chapter 3: Navigating Career Ambitions with AI Integration The integration of AI into the workplace has brought unprecedented changes to career dynamics. Automation and machine learning are transforming industries, creating new opportunities while rendering certain jobs obsolete. As professionals, we must adapt to this rapidly evolving landscape, acquiring new skills and embracing lifelong learning to stay relevant. Balancing career ambitions with the ethical considerations of AI implementation is crucial for sustainable success.

AI-driven tools can enhance productivity, streamline processes, and unlock new levels of innovation. However, they also raise questions about the future of work and the role of human creativity. As we delegate routine tasks to machines, our focus can shift towards more strategic and creative endeavors. This shift requires a reimagining of career paths, where adaptability and continuous improvement become the cornerstones of professional growth.

In this new paradigm, the importance of human-centric skills cannot be overstated. Emotional intelligence, empathy, and collaboration are qualities that AI cannot replicate. Cultivating these skills can set us apart in an increasingly automated world. Networking, mentorship, and building meaningful relationships within the workplace become essential for career advancement. By fostering a culture of collaboration and innovation, we can create environments where both humans and AI thrive.

Moreover, ethical considerations play a significant role in the integration of AI into our careers. As we harness the power of AI, we must ensure that its implementation aligns with our values and principles. Transparency, fairness, and accountability are essential in building trust and mitigating potential risks. By advocating for responsible AI practices, we can shape a future where technology serves humanity, rather than the other way around.

Chapter 4: Faith in an Age of Uncertainty In an age characterized by rapid technological advancements and constant change, the quest for spiritual fulfillment and faith takes on new significance. As we navigate the complexities of modern life, finding a sense of purpose and connection to something greater than ourselves becomes essential. AI can be a powerful tool for exploring and deepening our faith, but it also presents challenges that require discernment and mindfulness.

Digital platforms and AI-driven applications have revolutionized the way we access and engage with spiritual content. Online sermons, meditation apps, and virtual communities offer unprecedented opportunities for spiritual growth and connection. However, these technologies can also lead to a superficial approach to faith, where convenience takes precedence over genuine engagement. Balancing the benefits of technology with the need for authentic spiritual practices is crucial for nurturing a meaningful faith life.

The integration of AI into faith practices can also raise ethical and philosophical questions. As we rely on algorithms to guide our spiritual journeys, we must be vigilant in ensuring that these tools align with our values and beliefs. The potential for AI to shape and influence our spiritual experiences requires a critical and reflective approach. By maintaining a sense of agency and discernment, we can harness the power of AI while staying true to our spiritual principles.

Moreover, the communal aspect of faith remains vital in an increasingly digital world. While online communities can provide support and connection, they cannot fully replace the experience of shared worship and fellowship. Gathering in person, participating in rituals, and engaging in acts of service are essential components of a vibrant faith life. By balancing virtual engagement with real-world experiences, we can create a holistic and enriching spiritual practice.

Chapter 5: Balancing Personal and Professional Lives The integration of AI into both personal and professional realms has blurred the lines between work and home life. With remote work becoming increasingly common, maintaining a healthy work-life balance is more challenging than ever. AI-powered tools can help us manage our time and tasks more efficiently, but they also demand greater self-discipline and boundary-setting to prevent burnout and maintain well-being.

In this new reality, setting clear boundaries between work and personal life is essential. Establishing designated work hours, creating a dedicated workspace, and prioritizing self-care can help us navigate the demands of both domains. Leveraging AI-driven productivity tools can streamline tasks and enhance efficiency, allowing us to focus on what truly matters. However, it is crucial to remember that technology should serve us, not dominate our lives.

Moreover, the importance of meaningful relationships and social connections cannot be overstated. Balancing personal and professional lives requires nurturing relationships with family, friends, and colleagues. AI can facilitate communication and collaboration, but it cannot replace the value of face-to-face interactions and shared experiences. By investing time and effort in our relationships, we can create a support network that sustains us through life's challenges.

Additionally, pursuing passions and hobbies outside of work is essential for maintaining a balanced life. Engaging in activities that bring joy and fulfillment can recharge our spirits and enhance our overall well-being. AI can provide personalized recommendations and resources for pursuing our interests, but it is our responsibility to prioritize these activities and make time for them. By embracing a holistic approach to life, we can achieve a harmonious balance between our personal and professional aspirations.

Chapter 6: AI's Role in Mental Health and Well-being AI has the potential to revolutionize mental health care and well-being, offering innovative solutions for diagnosis, treatment, and support. AI-powered applications can provide personalized mental health resources, such as virtual therapy sessions, mood tracking, and mindfulness exercises. These tools can enhance accessibility and convenience, making mental health care more inclusive and widespread.

However, the integration of AI into mental health care also raises important considerations. While AI can offer valuable support, it cannot fully replace the expertise and empathy of human therapists. The human touch remains essential for building trust, understanding complex emotions, and providing nuanced care. Balancing the use of AI-driven tools with human interaction is crucial for effective mental health care.

Moreover, the ethical implications of AI in mental health care must be carefully considered. Issues such as data privacy, algorithmic bias, and informed consent are paramount in ensuring that AI applications are used responsibly and ethically. By advocating for transparent and accountable practices, we can harness the benefits of AI while safeguarding the rights and dignity of individuals seeking mental health support.

Additionally, promoting mental well-being in the age of AI requires a proactive and holistic approach. Incorporating mindfulness practices, self-care routines, and healthy lifestyle choices can enhance our resilience and overall mental health. AI can offer valuable resources and guidance, but it is our responsibility to take active steps towards nurturing our well-being. By embracing a balanced approach to mental health care, we can thrive in an increasingly digital world.

Chapter 7: The Future of Education and Lifelong Learning AI is transforming the landscape of education, creating new opportunities for personalized learning and lifelong skill development. Traditional classrooms are evolving, with AI-powered tools providing customized learning experiences tailored to individual needs and preferences. This shift is redefining how we acquire knowledge, fostering a culture of continuous learning and adaptability in an ever-changing world.

One of the most significant benefits of AI in education is its ability to provide personalized learning paths. Through data analysis and adaptive algorithms, AI can identify a student's strengths, weaknesses, and learning styles, offering targeted resources and support. This individualized approach can enhance student engagement, improve academic outcomes, and foster a love for learning. By embracing AI-driven education, we can create more inclusive and effective learning environments.

Lifelong learning has become a necessity in the age of AI, as the rapid pace of technological advancements requires continuous skill development. AI-powered platforms offer a wealth of resources for professional growth, from online courses and virtual workshops to interactive simulations and real-time feedback. These tools enable individuals to upskill and reskill, staying relevant in their careers and adapting to new challenges. By cultivating a mindset of lifelong learning, we can thrive in an AI-driven world.

Moreover, the role of educators is evolving alongside AI integration. Teachers and instructors are no longer mere transmitters of knowledge but facilitators of learning experiences. AI can support educators by automating administrative tasks, providing real-time insights into student progress, and offering tailored instructional materials. This shift allows educators to focus on fostering critical thinking, creativity, and emotional intelligence, preparing students for a future where human skills remain essential.

Chapter 8: Ethical Considerations in an AI-Driven Society As AI becomes increasingly integrated into our daily lives, ethical considerations take on heightened importance. The potential benefits of AI are vast, but they come with risks that must be carefully managed. Issues such as data privacy, algorithmic bias, and transparency are central to ensuring that AI serves humanity ethically and responsibly.

Data privacy is a critical concern in the age of AI. As we rely on AI-driven applications for various aspects of our lives, the amount of personal data collected and analyzed is unprecedented. Ensuring that this data is handled securely and transparently is essential to building trust in AI technologies. Privacy regulations and ethical guidelines must be enforced to protect individuals' rights and prevent misuse of personal information.

Algorithmic bias is another significant challenge in AI development. AI systems are only as unbiased as the data they are trained on, and if this data reflects societal biases, the algorithms can perpetuate and even amplify these biases. Addressing this issue requires a concerted effort to ensure diverse and representative datasets, as well as ongoing scrutiny and refinement of AI models. By prioritizing fairness and inclusivity, we can create AI systems that promote equity and social justice.

Transparency is fundamental to the ethical use of AI. Understanding how AI systems make decisions is crucial for accountability and trust. This requires clear communication about the algorithms' workings, the data used, and the potential implications of AI-driven decisions. By fostering a culture of transparency and ethical responsibility, we can harness the power of AI while mitigating its risks.

Chapter 9: Building Resilience in the Age of AI Resilience is a vital trait in navigating the complexities of an AI-driven world. The rapid pace of technological change can be overwhelming, but cultivating resilience can help us adapt and thrive. Building resilience involves developing a growth mindset, fostering emotional intelligence, and maintaining a strong support network.

A growth mindset is essential for embracing change and continuous learning. Viewing challenges as opportunities for growth rather than obstacles can help us stay motivated and resilient in the face of adversity. This mindset encourages us to seek out new experiences, take risks, and learn from failures. By embracing a growth mindset, we can navigate the uncertainties of the AI age with confidence and optimism.

Emotional intelligence plays a crucial role in building resilience. Understanding and managing our emotions, as well as empathizing with others, can help us navigate the complexities of human interactions in an increasingly digital world. Developing emotional intelligence involves self-awareness, self-regulation, and effective communication. These skills enable us to build meaningful relationships, manage stress, and maintain a positive outlook.

A strong support network is also essential for resilience. Surrounding ourselves with supportive and like-minded individuals can provide encouragement, guidance, and a sense of belonging. Whether through family, friends, or professional networks, having a community of support can help us navigate the challenges of the AI age. By fostering connections and seeking out positive relationships, we can build the resilience needed to thrive.

Chapter 10: Embracing Creativity and Innovation In an AI-driven world, creativity and innovation are more important than ever. While AI can enhance productivity and streamline processes, it is human creativity that drives meaningful innovation and progress. Embracing our creative potential can help us solve complex problems, adapt to new challenges, and envision a brighter future.

Creativity is a uniquely human trait that AI cannot replicate. It involves thinking outside the box, generating novel ideas, and seeing connections where others do not. Cultivating creativity requires an open mind, a willingness to experiment, and the ability to embrace uncertainty. By nurturing our creative potential, we can harness the power of AI to complement our innovative endeavors.

Innovation is the process of turning creative ideas into practical solutions. In the age of AI, innovation is not limited to technological advancements but extends to new ways of thinking, working, and living. AI can support innovation by providing tools for rapid prototyping, data analysis, and predictive modeling. However, it is human ingenuity and vision that drive transformative change.

Moreover, fostering a culture of creativity and innovation requires an environment that encourages risk-taking and experimentation. Organizations and communities that prioritize creativity can create spaces where individuals feel empowered to explore new ideas and challenge the status quo. By embracing a culture of creativity and innovation, we can unlock the full potential of both human and AI capabilities.

Chapter 11: The Role of Community in an AI-Driven World Community plays a vital role in navigating the complexities of an AI-driven world. As technology reshapes our lives, the importance of human connections and social support becomes even more pronounced. Building and nurturing strong communities can provide a sense of belonging, purpose, and resilience in the face of change.

AI can enhance community building by facilitating communication, collaboration, and access to resources. Online platforms and social networks can connect individuals across geographical boundaries, creating virtual communities based on shared interests and values. These digital communities can provide support, knowledge, and a sense of belonging. However, it is essential to balance online interactions with real-world connections to maintain a sense of authenticity and depth in our relationships.

Local communities also play a crucial role in fostering social cohesion and resilience. Engaging in community activities, volunteering, and participating in local initiatives can strengthen our sense of belonging and contribute to the well-being of others. By building strong local networks, we can create supportive environments where individuals feel valued and connected.

Moreover, the role of community extends to addressing the ethical and societal implications of AI. Engaging in open dialogue and collaborative decision-making can ensure that AI technologies are developed and implemented in ways that align with our shared values and principles. By fostering a sense of collective responsibility, we can shape a future where AI serves the common good.

Chapter 12: Finding Balance and Fulfillment in the AI Age Finding balance and fulfillment in the age of AI requires a holistic approach that encompasses love, career, faith, and well-being. Embracing the opportunities presented by AI while staying true to our human values and connections is essential for a fulfilling life. By prioritizing what truly matters, we can navigate the complexities of the AI age with grace and purpose.

Balancing love and relationships in the digital age involves maintaining authenticity and emotional intimacy in our interactions. While AI can facilitate connections, it is our responsibility to nurture meaningful relationships through open communication, vulnerability, and shared experiences. By prioritizing love and connection, we can create fulfilling relationships that withstand the test of time.

In our careers, balancing ambition with ethical considerations and continuous learning is key to success. Leveraging AI's capabilities while preserving human creativity and empathy can help us thrive in an evolving job market. By cultivating a growth mindset and staying adaptable, we can pursue our professional goals with integrity and resilience.

Faith and spirituality provide a sense of purpose and connection to something greater than ourselves. In the age of AI, maintaining a mindful and authentic approach to faith practices is essential. Balancing digital engagement with real-world experiences can create a holistic and enriching spiritual life.

Ultimately, finding balance and fulfillment in the AI age involves embracing our human potential while leveraging the power of technology. By prioritizing love, career, faith, and well-being, we can create a harmonious and meaningful life. In this ever-changing world, staying true to our values and connections will guide us towards a future where both humanity and AI can thrive.

Chapter 13: AI and Global Collaboration In an interconnected world, AI has the potential to foster global collaboration and address some of humanity's most pressing challenges. From climate change to healthcare, AI-driven solutions can facilitate cross-border cooperation and resource sharing. By leveraging AI's capabilities, we can pool our collective knowledge and expertise to create innovative solutions that transcend geographical boundaries.

AI-powered platforms can connect researchers, policymakers, and organizations from around the world, enabling them to collaborate on projects and share insights in real-time. This global exchange of ideas can accelerate progress and drive meaningful change. However, it is essential to ensure that these collaborations are built on principles of equity, inclusivity, and mutual respect. By fostering a culture of global cooperation, we can harness the power of AI to create a more just and sustainable world.

Moreover, AI can play a pivotal role in addressing global health disparities. AI-driven diagnostics, predictive modeling, and telemedicine can enhance access to healthcare in underserved regions. By leveraging AI's capabilities, we can develop cost-effective and scalable solutions that improve health outcomes for vulnerable populations. However, it is crucial to address ethical considerations and ensure that AI technologies are used responsibly and equitably.

Additionally, AI can contribute to global efforts to combat climate change and protect the environment. AI-powered tools can analyze vast amounts of data to identify patterns and predict environmental trends. These insights can inform policy decisions, optimize resource management, and drive sustainable practices. By collaborating on AI-driven environmental initiatives, we can work towards a healthier and more resilient planet.

Chapter 14: The Art of Mindful Technology Use In an era dominated by technology, mindful use of AI and digital devices is essential for maintaining well-being and balance. The constant connectivity and information overload can lead to stress, anxiety, and a sense of disconnection from the present moment. Embracing mindfulness in our interactions with technology can help us cultivate a healthier relationship with digital tools and enhance our overall quality of life.

Mindful technology use involves being intentional about how and when we engage with digital devices. Setting boundaries, such as designated tech-free times and spaces, can help us create a sense of balance and prevent burnout. Taking regular breaks from screens and engaging in activities that promote relaxation and presence, such as meditation or spending time in nature, can enhance our mental and emotional well-being.

Additionally, practicing digital detox can provide valuable opportunities for reflection and rejuvenation. Disconnecting from digital devices for a set period can help us reset our minds and reconnect with ourselves and our surroundings. By incorporating regular digital detoxes into our routine, we can cultivate a sense of clarity and focus.

Moreover, fostering a mindful approach to technology use involves being conscious of the content we consume and how it impacts us. Curating our digital environment to prioritize positive and uplifting content can enhance our well-being. Engaging in online activities that promote connection, creativity, and personal growth can help us make the most of our digital experiences while maintaining a sense of balance.

Chapter 15: AI and the Future of Creativity AI's influence on creativity and the arts is a fascinating and evolving landscape. From AI-generated music and art to virtual reality experiences, technology is pushing the boundaries of what is possible in creative expression. While AI can enhance and augment human creativity, it also raises questions about authorship, originality, and the nature of artistic creation.

AI-powered tools can serve as valuable collaborators in the creative process, offering new perspectives and possibilities. For example, AI algorithms can analyze vast datasets to identify patterns and generate novel ideas that inspire artists and creators. These tools can assist in brainstorming, refining concepts, and even creating entire works of art. By embracing AI as a creative partner, we can unlock new realms of innovation and artistic exploration.

However, the integration of AI into the creative process also requires careful consideration of ethical and philosophical questions. The question of authorship becomes complex when AI-generated works blur the lines between human and machine contributions. Additionally, concerns about the impact of AI on traditional artistic practices and livelihoods must be addressed. By fostering open dialogue and ethical practices, we can navigate the evolving relationship between AI and creativity.

Moreover, AI's role in creativity extends to making the arts more accessible and inclusive. AI-powered platforms can democratize access to creative tools and resources, enabling individuals from diverse backgrounds to express themselves and share their work with the world. This inclusivity can lead to a richer and more diverse cultural landscape, where a multitude of voices and perspectives are represented.

Chapter 16: AI and the Evolution of Human Identity The integration of AI into our lives is reshaping our understanding of human identity and selfhood. As we interact with AI-driven technologies, questions about what it means to be human and the nature of consciousness come to the forefront. Navigating this evolving landscape requires reflection and introspection, as we explore the intersections of technology, identity, and self-expression.

AI has the potential to enhance our self-understanding and self-expression. AI-powered tools can analyze our behaviors, preferences, and patterns, offering insights that help us better understand ourselves. These insights can inform personal growth, self-improvement, and well-being. However, it is crucial to approach these tools with a sense of agency and discernment, ensuring that they serve as complements to our self-exploration rather than determinants of our identity.

Additionally, the digital age offers new avenues for self-expression and identity formation. Social media, virtual reality, and AI-driven platforms provide spaces for individuals to explore and present different facets of their identities. While these platforms can facilitate connection and creativity, they also raise questions about authenticity and the impact of digital personas on our sense of self. By fostering mindful and intentional use of these technologies, we can navigate the complexities of digital identity with integrity.

Moreover, the evolving relationship between humans and AI invites us to reflect on the nature of consciousness and the boundaries of human experience. As AI systems become more sophisticated, the distinctions between human and machine intelligence may become increasingly blurred. Engaging with these questions can deepen our understanding of what it means to be human and inspire new ways of thinking about consciousness, creativity, and selfhood.

Chapter 17: Embracing the Unknown and Shaping the Future As we journey through the age of AI, embracing the unknown and shaping the future with intention and purpose becomes paramount. The rapid pace of technological change can be both exhilarating and daunting, but it also presents opportunities for growth, innovation, and transformation. By approaching the future with curiosity, resilience, and a sense of responsibility, we can navigate the uncertainties of the AI age with confidence and optimism.

Embracing the unknown involves cultivating a sense of curiosity and openness to new experiences and possibilities. Viewing challenges as opportunities for learning and growth can help us adapt and thrive in an ever-changing world. By maintaining a flexible and adaptive mindset, we can navigate the complexities of the AI age with agility and creativity.

Moreover, shaping the future with intention requires a commitment to ethical principles and values. As we harness the power of AI, we must ensure that its development and implementation align with our vision for a just, inclusive, and sustainable world. Engaging in responsible AI practices, advocating for transparency and accountability, and prioritizing the common good can guide us towards a future where technology serves humanity.

Additionally, fostering a sense of collective responsibility and collaboration is essential for shaping the future. By working together, we can address the challenges and opportunities of the AI age, creating a world where both humans and AI thrive. Building strong communities, promoting global cooperation, and embracing diversity and inclusivity can help us navigate the complexities of the AI age and create a brighter future for all.

Ultimately, the journey through the age of AI is one of continuous exploration, reflection, and growth. By balancing love, career, faith, and well-being, we can navigate the complexities of the AI age with grace and purpose. In this ever-evolving world, staying true to our values and connections will guide us towards a future where both humanity and AI can thrive.

Book Description:

In a world where artificial intelligence is woven into the fabric of our daily lives, we are faced with profound questions about love, career, and faith. **"Code of the Heart: Balancing Love, Career, and Faith in the Age of AI"** delves into the intricate interplay between technology and the human experience. This insightful and thought-provoking book explores how AI reshapes our most fundamental aspects of existence, and offers guidance on maintaining a harmonious balance in this new era.

Through 17 chapters, readers embark on a journey that navigates the complexities of modern love, from the convenience and challenges of digital dating to the deeper connections that transcend screens. The book examines the impact of AI on our careers, highlighting the importance of adaptability, continuous learning, and ethical considerations in an evolving job market. It also addresses the role of faith and spirituality in an age of uncertainty, exploring how technology can both enhance and challenge our spiritual practices.

"Code of the Heart" emphasizes the importance of resilience, creativity, and community in navigating the AI age. It offers practical strategies for mindful technology use, maintaining meaningful relationships, and embracing lifelong learning. With a focus on ethical responsibility and global collaboration, the book invites readers to shape a future where both humanity and AI can thrive.

Engaging, insightful, and deeply human, "Code of the Heart" is a must-read for anyone seeking to find balance and fulfillment in an AI-driven world. Whether you are navigating the complexities of love, career, or faith, this book provides valuable insights and inspiration for living a harmonious and purpose-driven life.

www.ingramcontent.com/pod-product-compliance
Lightning Source LLC
LaVergne TN
LVHW020510080526
838202LV00057B/6272